EXTREME WEATHER

Margaret Hynes

KINGFISHER
NEW YORK

KINGFISHER
LONDON & NEW YORK

Copyright © Kingfisher 2011
Published in the United States by Kingfisher,
175 Fifth Ave., New York, NY 10010
Kingfisher is an imprint of Macmillan Children's Books, London.
All rights reserved.

Distributed in the U.S. by Macmillan,
175 Fifth Ave., New York, NY 10010

Library of Congress Cataloging-in-Publication data has been applied for.

ISBN 978-0-7534-6578-3

Consultant: Dr. Mike Goldsmith

Illustrations by: The Peter Bull Art Studio—Peter Bull
The Art Agency—Mick Posen, Mark Garlick
Linden Artists—Steve & Sam Weston, Seb Quigley

Kingfisher books are available for special promotions and premiums.
For details contact: Special Markets Department, Macmillan, 175 Fifth Ave., New York, NY 10010.

For more information, please visit www.kingfisherbooks.com

Printed in China
1 3 5 7 9 8 6 4 2
1TR/0311/UG/WKT/140MA

**The Publisher would like to thank the following for permission to reproduce their material. Every care has been taken to trace copyright holders.
However, if there have been unintentional omissions or failure to trace copyright holders, we apologize and will, if informed, endeavor to make
corrections in any future edition (t = top, b = bottom, c = center, r = right, l = left):**

Cover: Shutterstock/1000 Words; back cover: Alamy/Tom Viggers

Page 4tr Getty/Stephen Jaffe; 4bc Corbis/Theo Allofs; 5tc Corbis/epa; 5cl Press Association(PA)/AP; 5cr Nature PL/Marguerite Smits van Oyen; 5bl Frank Lane Picture Agency (FLPA)/Frans Lanting;
6 NASA/JPL/ISS; 7 Shutterstock/Susie Prentice; 8cr Corbis/Jim Reed; 9tl Shutterstock/Jhaz Photography; 9tc NASA/JPL/ISS; 9 Photolibrary/Peter Arnold Images; 9bc Corbis/Jim Reed; 10–11 Corbis/Wallace
Garrison/Monsoon; 10tc Corbis/Matt Sullivan/Reuters; 10tc Shutterstock/Jhaz Photography; 10tr Alamy/Thierry Grun; 11tr Science Photo Library (SPL)/Peter Menzel; 11cr Shutterstock/Image Team; 11bc
Corbis/Scott Stulberg; 12–13 Alamy/A. T. Willett; 12tr Corbis/Jim Reed/Science Faction; 12c Shutterstock/Franc Podgorsek; 12bl Shutterstock/Alexander Ozerov; 13t Corbis/David Crosling; 13tr Reuters/China
Photos; 13b Corbis/Wojtek Kaminski; 14 Shutterstock/Dark o; 15tc SPL/Jim Reed; 15r SPL/Howard Bluestein; 16c Alamy/Kevin Howchin; 18–19 Getty/AFP; 18c PA/AP; 19tr PA/Dav Raj Pant/AP; 19cl Getty/Sean
Gallup; 19br PA Wire/Barry Batechelor/AP; 20tl PA/Robert F. Bukaty/AP; 20 Shutterstock/Antonio S.; 20br Shutterstock/Demid; 20cr Corbis/Henrik Trygg; 20tr Corbis/Larry W. Smith; 21cl Getty/Dan Rafla/Aurora;
21c Blue Green Images; 21b Shutterstock/Four Oaks; 21r Getty/Franz Aberham; 22tr Getty/Adrian Pope; 22c PA/Rajes Kumar Singh/AP; 22bl Alamy/RADIANCE; 23br PA/AP; 24 Getty/National Geographic
Society; 25c Getty/Imagebank; 25tr Corbis/Kazuyoshi Nomachi; 26cl Corbis/Bob E. Daemmrich; 26tr Trevor/Met. Office Australia; 26b SPL/NASA; 26–27t NASA; 27 SPL/NASA; 27bl Shutterstock/Seti; 27br
Corbis/Reuters; 28–29 NASA/JPL; 29tl Getty/Ted Soqui/Flickr; 29c Getty/AFP; 29cr PA/AP; 29bl Reuters/Tim Wimbourne; 29br Shutterstock/Melvin Lee; 30 Shutterstock/dinadesign; 32 Corbis/Steve Kaufman;
33 Getty/Mandel Ngan; 34–35 Shutterstock/kavram; 34cr Corbis/Christine Schneider; 34br Alamy/imagebroker; 35tc Shutterstock/Lars Lindblad; 35c Shutterstock/vesilvio; 35bc WaterAid/Newah; 35bl
Photolibrary/John Woodworth; 36–37 NASA; 36tr SPL/Jim Reed; 36bl SPL/SFR; 36bc NOAA; 37t NOAA; 37c Corbis/Jim Edds/Jim Reed; 38cl Shutterstock/cardiae; 38t, 38–39, and 39tl NASA; 39c Corbis/Ashley
Cooper; 39cr SPL/British Antarctic Survey; 40tl Getty/ChinaFotoPress; 40tc Corbis/Najlah Feanny; 40tr PA/AP/David J. Phillip; 40c Getty/UN.MINUSTAH; 40br PA/AP; 41 PA/AP; 41bc PA/AP/Paloa Crociana;
42tr Alamy/Photoshot; 42bl Corbis/Frederic Soltan; 42br Photoshot/Shafiqul Islam/WpN; 43tl Alamy/David Gordon; 43tr Corbis/Skyscan; 43bl Alamy/StockShot; 43br Getty/AFP; 48tr Alamy/Jeff Greenberg;
48cl Alamy/David R. Frazier Photolibrary; 48cr Getty/Time & Life Pictures/Ted Russell; 48bl Alamy/Arcticphoto; 48bl Shutterstock/Ilona Baha

CONTENTS

ATMOSPHERE—the giant blanket of air surrounding Earth

WEATHER WORLD

You may not realize it, but weather has a huge influence on your life. It affects what you wear, the type of house you live in, and the food you eat. Weather is the condition of the lowest level of the atmosphere, called the troposphere, at a given time and place. Weather is determined by such things as temperature, air pressure, humidity, and wind. While weather whips up waves at sea and even carves rocks over time, extremes of weather are more fearsome, creating many of the world's worst disasters.

1

The fierce, twisting winds of a tornado flatten everything in their path.

2

"If you spend your whole life waiting for the storm, you'll never enjoy the sunshine."

Morris West (1916–1999)
Australian novelist

Drought

Around the world, different areas receive different amounts of rain. When an area receives much less rain than usual, or no rain at all, the region experiences a drought. During a drought, once-fertile soil may turn to dust and rivers may dry up, leaving only a cracked riverbed.

Extreme conditions

While tropical regions roast under the searing sun, polar regions freeze under a thick layer of ice. The hot, moist weather of some areas builds savage storms, such as hurricanes and tornadoes. Heavy rainfall can lead to floods and unusually low rainfall causes droughts. Hazards in cold parts of the world include blizzards and avalanches.

> Meteorologists (weather scientists) issued the first-ever weather forecasts in 1869 in the United States.

Some farmers wear woven rain shields, called krups, as protection against the relentless rain, and so that they can keep their hands free for working.

An avalanche's rolling mass of snow engulfs a ski chalet in the European Alps.

Penguins huddle together for warmth during Antarctic blizzards.

Salt miners work in the relatively cooler mornings and evenings rather than in the baking heat of the middle of the day.

KEY

1 Known as Tornado Alley, this part of the U.S. has more tornadoes than anywhere else on Earth.

2 The Atacama Desert, South America, contains sites that are the driest places on our planet.

3 The European Alps can suffer from avalanches during heavy snowfall.

4 Antarctica is the coldest and windiest place on Earth.

5 Afar depression, Ethiopia, is the hottest inhabited place in the world.

6 Cherrapunji, India, is among the wettest places on Earth.

WEATHER MACHINE

Earth's weather is controlled by the Sun. It heats air masses in different parts of the globe, making them lighter and causing them to rise through the atmosphere. Cool air rushes in to fill the gap, and we feel this movement of air as wind. The heat of the Sun also helps water vapor form and move to create rain, snow, or thunderstorms. Earth is heated unevenly by the Sun, but global winds and ocean currents redistribute the heat around the world, helping prevent severe extremes of temperature.

Atmospheric pressure

Air pressure is greatest near the ground, because there is a larger weight of air pushing down from above. The higher in the atmosphere you go, the less air and air pressure there is.

The Sun's rays hit the poles at an angle.

Earth is tilted at an angle of 23.5 degrees.

The Sun's rays hit Earth at different angles.

Solar power

The power of sunlight that a region receives depends on the angle at which the Sun hits it. Toward the poles, the Sun's rays come in at such a shallow angle that they are spread out and weakened, which is why polar regions are cold. But in the tropics, the rays can strike from directly overhead, so tropical regions are warm. During the day, the Sun is weakest at dusk and dawn, when it sets and rises. It is at its strongest in the middle of the day, when it shines down most directly.

KEY

the polar regions, where it is cold

the tropics, where it is warm

the equator, where it is hot

The side of the globe facing away from the Sun is in darkness.

 > The Sun's core temperature is 27 million °F (15 million °C), and its surface temperature is 10,000°F (5,500°C).

"The Earth has received the embrace of the Sun, and we shall see the results of that love."

Sitting Bull (c. 1831–1890)
Hunkpapa Lakota Sioux leader and holy man

The Sun's rays hit the equator straight on.

⊖ MOVING WATER AND AIR

Water cycle

Moisture rises up from Earth's surface and falls back down again in a never-ending cycle driven by the Sun's energy. As the Sun heats the surface of lakes and oceans, moisture evaporates, turning into an invisible gas called water vapor. This rises into the air, where cooler temperatures high up cause the water vapor to condense as clouds and then to fall back to Earth as rain, snow, or hail.

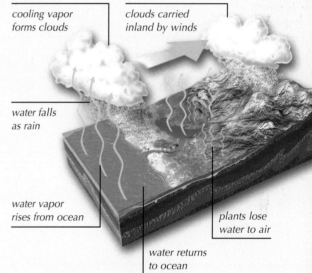

cooling vapor forms clouds

clouds carried inland by winds

water falls as rain

water vapor rises from ocean

plants lose water to air

water returns to ocean

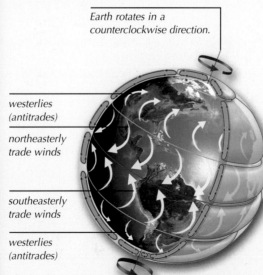

Earth rotates in a counterclockwise direction.

westerlies (antitrades)

northeasterly trade winds

southeasterly trade winds

westerlies (antitrades)

World winds

Together, the Sun's heat and Earth's rotation create global patterns of wind. Moist air at the equator, warmed by the Sun, rises into the atmosphere. It then spreads north and south, dropping most of its moisture over the wet tropics. Farther north and south, the now-dry air sinks, creating dry conditions. Some of the air flows back to the equator. The rest flows toward the poles until it meets cold, polar air. The warmer air rises again and recirculates into the atmosphere.

The Southern Hemisphere is tilted toward the Sun, which means it is summer there.

THUNDEROUS STORMS

You can be sure it will rain if dark, gray clouds fill the sky. The clouds are dark because they are so full of water that sunlight cannot pass through them. If the clouds grow into a giant anvil shape with a dark, flat base, topped by columns of lighter clouds, a thunderstorm is on the way. Such clouds are called cumulonimbus, and they generate a huge amount of energy, which is released in the form of updrafts and bursts of electricity. Storm clouds produce thunder, lightning, strong winds, and heavy rain or snow.

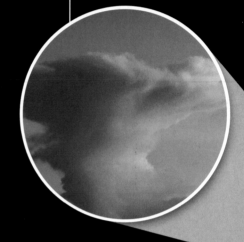

The top, which is made from ice crystals because the air is colder at this height, is swept into a huge anvil shape by the wind.

Supercell

Most thunderstorms develop from updrafts, or cells of rising air. Particularly large and energetic, rotating updrafts—in which air rises more quickly than normal—are called supercells. These carry a huge amount of water up into a thundercloud. Supercells produce tornadoes and waterspouts.

BIRTH OF A STORM CLOUD

Warm, moist air rises and cools, causing its water vapor to condense into droplets that form a cumulus cloud. Condensation releases latent heat, which makes the air rise farther and the cloud grow taller. When the droplets in the cloud become heavy enough to fall, precipitation begins and the air cools, causing a downdraft that breaks up the cloud.

1. Warm updrafts rise to create cumulus clouds.

2. The cold rain, snow, or hail drags air down with it, creating a cold downdraft.

3. When there is more downdraft than updraft, the cloud dissolves (breaks up).

> About 45,000 thunderstorms hit different parts of Earth each day.

The clouds stop rising and spread out as they hit a cold, dry layer of air.

Thunderclouds

A cumulonimbus cloud can reach 10 mi. (16km) or more in the air, while its base may loom only 1,650 ft. (500m) above the ground. The air inside these clouds rises and sinks in currents, traveling at 30 mph (50km/h) or more. Aircraft pilots steer clear of thunderclouds because the fierce currents can catapult an aircraft upward and downward, which could possibly cause the pilots to lose control of the aircraft.

giant cumulonimbus clouds

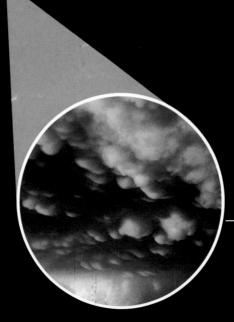

Mammatus clouds often form on the undersides of cumulonimbus clouds, but scientists cannot agree on how they are formed.

ELECTRIC SKIES

When the ominous shape of a giant cumulonimbus looms, it does not take long before the sky erupts into a spectacle of zigzagging flashing light, deafening noise, and pouring rain. It looks magnificent, but lightning is also very dangerous. Around the world, about 200 people per year are killed by lightning strikes. Lightning is a huge surge of electricity. It heats the air to about 54,000°F (30,000°C), which is five times hotter than the surface of the Sun. This superheating of the air is heard as thunder.

"Thunder is good, thunder is impressive; but it is lightning that does all the work."

Mark Twain (1835–1910)
American novelist

Sporting strikes

Humans are 65 percent water, which conducts electricity well. As a result, people standing on golf courses or other exposed sites are good targets for lightning.

Lighter, positively charged pieces of ice and water droplets are driven up toward the top of the cloud.

Great balls of fire

Sometimes, during thundery weather, a curious ball of lightning appears a few yards above the ground and then bounces around randomly. Scientists cannot agree on how this ball lightning is formed.

Heavier, negatively charged water droplets and pieces of ice build up at the base of the cloud.

Lightning bolts begin when a small stroke, known as a leader stroke, zigzags to the ground.

Lightning flashes within the cloud are called sheet lightning.

Lightning generator

Air currents inside a cumulonimbus cloud cause ice crystals or water droplets within the cloud to crash into one another, creating electrical charges—like rubbing a balloon against your hair. The bottom of the cloud becomes negatively charged. The ground and cloud top are positively charged. These charges build up, and when the difference is big enough, electricity darts around. At first, lightning flashes are created inside the cloud. Then, bolts of lightning dart from the cloud to the ground.

> CONDUCTOR—*a substance that allows electricity to pass through it easily*

TURNED TO STONE

A bolt of lightning can heat the ground to about 3,300°F (1,800°C) in less than one 100,000th of a second. If a bolt of lightning strikes dry sand, it melts and fuses the sand in the electricity's path. Once it cools, the molten sand can form strange, tubular, branchlike formations called fulgurites. The outer surfaces of fulgurites are often covered with unfused sand grains, which creates a texture like sandpaper. The inner surfaces are usually smooth and glassy.

a cooled and hardened fulgurite, created from sand fused by a lightning strike

A huge surge of lightning, known as a return stroke, shoots up the path created by the leader stroke.

The ground is positively charged.

Lightning conductors

Lightning tends to strike tall objects, so skyscrapers are struck regularly. Most have metal rods called lightning conductors on their roofs. The rods protect the building by conducting the electricity safely to the ground.

Never take shelter under a tree during a storm. The moist layer beneath a tree's bark acts as a conductor, making trees vulnerable to lightning strikes.

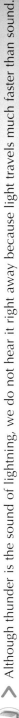

› Although thunder is the sound of lightning, we do not hear it right away because light travels much faster than sound.

ICY FALLS

Dodging hard lumps of ice hurtling from the sky at up to 105 mph (170km/h) is not easy—hailstones pelt anything and everything in the vicinity. They form when winds toss up ice crystals above the freezing level in a thundercloud and down again. Each time the ice rises, a new layer of ice forms around it. The more turbulent the storm cloud, the larger the hailstone becomes before it falls to the ground. Most hailstorms unleash pea-size hailstones, but some produce ice lumps the size of grapefruits.

This cross section of a hailstone reveals its internal structure of alternating layers of ice. Each layer represents a roundtrip to the top of a storm cloud and back down again.

car roof is severely dented by falling ice

people and cars making their way through a violent hailstorm in Sydney, Australia

hailstones smash straight through windshield

Crushed crops

Vast regions of cropland in the U.S., China, Russia, and other parts of Europe are under constant threat of damage from hailstorms. Here, pea-size hailstones have flattened a crop of gourds.

Hail havoc

Umbrellas offer little protection against pounding hailstones the size of golf balls. Such hailstones are strong enough to wipe out crops, damage buildings, cars, and aircraft, and seriously injure people. This is what happened in Sydney in 1999 during the most financially costly natural disaster in Australian history.

 ❯ The largest hailstone on record was 7 in. (17.8cm) in diameter and had a circumference of 18.7 in. (47.6cm).

Hailstones fall when they grow so big that their weight overcomes the strength of the storm's updrafts.

⊖ CLOUD BUSTER

Some farmers have taken nature in their own hands by using a technique called cloud seeding to reduce the size of hailstones falling onto their crops. The farmers employ scientists to rocket chemicals into the air to create cores from which extra hailstones develop. The air becomes so full of hailstones that none of them can grow large enough to cause serious damage to the crops.

preparing to fire hail-suppression chemicals in China

www.squidoo.com/hailstones

WATERSPOUT

Tornadoes that travel across an ocean or lake form swirling waterspouts. These can be a hazard to small boats, and they can cause saltwater rain to fall if they sweep onto land. One may look like a spout of water being sucked up to the storm cloud, but only about 3 ft. (1m) of water is lifted. The rest of the waterspout is formed of cloud.

A waterspout swirls across the ocean.

"When a tornado strikes, all of us are at risk."

Spencer Bachus (born 1947)
American politician

Fish in lakes are lifted up with the water by the high-pressure winds.

> VORTEX—*the motion of air or a fluid swirling rapidly around a central point*

Violent vortex

Winds around the destructive vortex (spinning center) of a tornado can move at up to 300 mph (500km/h). They lift the roofs off houses and blow cars, people, and animals around as if they were toys. The funnel winds, and the debris caught up in them, work like a circular saw, cutting up anything with which they make contact.

All the dust and broken objects picked up by the tornado give it a dark and menacing color.

Special Doppler radar dishes mounted on the back of trucks help scientists see whether a vortex is forming within a cloud.

People in areas that experience many tornadoes have underground shelters or reinforced rooms at home for protection.

THE TWISTER

If you see a swirling funnel of air descend from the base of a supercell storm cloud, get ready to witness the most extreme of all storms—a tornado—charging across the land. Tornadoes, also known as "twisters," form when warm air is drawn in at the base of the cloud and rises upward. As the air rises, it spins. If the spin is intense enough, the rotating air extends below the cloud base as a funnel. Tornadoes occur in North America, western Europe, eastern Asia, and Australia.

❯ The Tri-State Tornado of 1925 killed 695 people, making it the deadliest tornado in American history.

www.nssl.noaa.gov/edu/safety/tornadoguide.html

EYE WALL—a ring of cumulonimbus clouds that surrounds the eye of a tropical cyclone

stage one

stage two

The pressure falls as the storms start to grow and merge. As air flows toward the low-pressure zone, it picks up more energy from the warm ocean surface and also starts to spin in a counterclockwise direction.

High-level winds spiral outward, blowing clockwise.

The system takes on a circular shape once the thunderstorms merge.

Birth of a cyclone

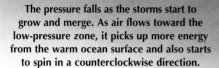

Tropical cyclones begin as small thunderstorms that form because the hot, tropical Sun evaporates water over the ocean. If the seawater is warmer than about 80°F (27°C), several storms may cluster together and whirl around as one. The storm system grows stronger, fueled by the warm surface water. Eventually, an area of calm—called the eye—develops at the center and the system becomes a cyclone. When cyclones move away from the warm water, they lose their source of energy and the winds drop rapidly.

"Anyone who says they're not afraid at the time of a hurricane is either a fool or a liar, or a little bit of both."

Anderson Cooper (born 1967)
American journalist and author

TROPICAL CYCLONES

Storm surge

Hurricane winds pile up water on the ocean's surface. In addition, the storm's eye pulls up a mound of water in the calm center of the storm. These bulges in the ocean are called storm surges, and they cause flooding if they reach land.

Furious, spiraling storms—which may be hundreds of miles across and with wind speeds of up to about 190 mph (300km/h)—develop in the tropical areas of oceans. These storms have different names in different parts of the world, but cyclones, hurricanes, and typhoons are all the same weather feature. If they cross onto the shore, it can spell disaster. This is because they can bring towering waves, torrential rain, and high winds that destroy buildings, cause massive flooding, and kill many people.

 > In 1970, Bhola cyclone struck Bangladesh and killed up to one million people—the deadliest tropical cyclone ever.

stage three

Cold, dry air descends in the eye, leaving it clear of cloud.

Whether tropical cyclones spin counterclockwise or clockwise depends on whether they are in the Northern or Southern Hemisphere.

The deadliest winds and most intense rainfall occur at the eye wall.

Warm, moist air spirals up around the wall of the hurricane's eye.

Winds at the water's surface blow counterclockwise.

Water vapor rises up from the ocean to form walls of clouds.

⊖ HURRICANE HIERARCHY

Scientists grade hurricanes from one to five according to their wind speed. The different categories cause different levels of damage when the storms reach land. A number one storm causes mild damage, while the worst storm, a number five hurricane, causes almost total destruction.

category one
wind: 74–95 mph
(119–153km/h)

category two

category three

category four

category five wind:
more than 155 mph (249km/h)

AFTERMATH

For people caught up in an extreme weather event, the passage of the weather itself does not always signal the end of their woes. Floods resulting from heavy rainfall, melting snow, or storm waves swamping a coast can cause widespread devastation and account for almost half of all deaths from natural disasters around the world. Heavy rains can also lead to deadly mudslides.

Rising river

A torrential downpour of rain caused this river in Dazhou, China, to fill beyond its capacity. The surplus water has overflowed the banks and is deluging buildings and streets, while the bridge is in danger of being swept away by the rising water.

Poor defenses

As Hurricane Katrina charged across the Gulf of Mexico in August 2005, the most severe loss of life occurred in New Orleans, Louisiana. This was because the storm surge caused by the hurricane broke through the levee system there, leading to flooding in about 80 percent of the city.

▽ LEVEE—a raised, sloping embankment that is built along a river on a coast as protection against flooding

> About 850,000 houses were damaged or destroyed in the New Orleans flood that followed Hurricane Katrina.

www.pbs.org/newshour/infocus/Floods/floods/science.html

Flood damage

These people are working hard to build defenses against rising floodwater because they know the havoc it could cause. Floods can destroy buildings, roads, and bridges, as well as cutting off services such as electricity and telephones. If sewage washes into drinking water supplies, deadly waterborne diseases, such as cholera and typhoid fever, can spread throughout flooded communities.

About 25,000 people took refuge inside the Louisiana Superdome.

⊖ MUDSLIDES

During very heavy rainfall, rainwater mixes with soil and forms mud. If this happens on a slope, gravity can pull the mud downward. This creates a moving river of mud known as a mudslide. Some mudslides begin quickly and continue like an avalanche, sweeping away people and buildings in their path. Nepal, in southern Asia, is especially prone to mudslides because the country is set on the slopes of the Himalayas, and monsoon rains drench it every year.

mudslide in Dadeldhura, Nepal, in 2009

"Great floods have flown from simple sources."

William Shakespeare (1564–1616)
English playwright,
from his play All's Well That Ends Well

Flash flood

If huge amounts of rain fall during a short period of time, a flash flood could strike. These are the most dangerous floods of all because they happen with hardly any warning, leaving people little time to protect themselves and their property. In 2004, a 10-ft.- (3-m)-high torrent of water surged through Boscastle, England, when about 2.5 in. (6.5cm) of rain fell in just two hours.

Thousands of buildings were submerged during the flood.

Trees were uprooted and cars were upturned by the torrent of water.

AIR-SEA
RESCUE

Winds disturb the surface of oceans, whipping up waves or twisting columns of spray into waterspouts. During severe storms, winds can push waves to heights of up to 100 ft. (30m). Boats at sea may be capsized (overturned) or wrecked by storm waves, which batter anything in their path when they crash onto the coast. It is often in these tempestuous conditions that seafarers find themselves in need of rescue.

Storm waves washed away the beach and damaged the road and houses.

Ship out of water

A storm surge can wrench boats from their moorings and smash them into one another. Sometimes, surging seawater carries boats far inland, leaving them high and dry when the water drains away.

High sea

With poor visibility and the distraction of crashing waves buffeting their vessel, lifeboat crews would find it difficult enough to stay afloat and keep themselves safe during a storm without also having to rescue others. In stormy conditions such as these, helicopters are deployed instead of boats. Once on the scene, the rescuer is lowered from the hovering helicopter on a winch lift to reach the person in trouble. The survivor is then attached to the rescuer and lifted up into the helicopter, which flies directly to a hospital.

> HIGH SEA—a very rough ocean, due to strong winds and storms

"The fishermen know that the sea is dangerous and the storm terrible, but they have never found those dangers sufficient reason for remaining ashore."

Vincent van Gogh (1853–1890)
Dutch artist

KEY

1. helicopter hovering in safety several yards above the crashing waves
2. winch operator winding up the winch lift
3. injured sailor being winched to safety and medical attention
4. waves buffeting a capsized boat
5. capsized sailor using the daggerboard to pull her sailing dinghy upright in the water
6. waves gouging out a cave in coastal rocks
7. submerged rocks onto which vessels could be forced during a storm

Giant waves can overwhelm a boat and cause it to capsize.

> The first air-sea rescue was carried out in 1911 by Hugh Robinson, who used his seaplane to pull a crashed pilot from Lake Michigan.

http://oceanservice.noaa.gov/education/kits/currents/03coastal1.html

MONSOONS

Monsoons are strong, sometimes violent winds that change direction with the seasons. Land warms up more quickly than the ocean, so continents are warmer than oceans in the summer. In the winter, the land gets cold more quickly than the ocean, which holds on to its heat for longer. Warm air rises, drawing in wind, so monsoon winds blow from the land toward the ocean in the winter and from the ocean toward the land in the summer. The most prominent monsoons occur in southern Asia, Africa, Australia, and the Pacific Coast.

JET STREAM—*fast-flowing air currents that circle Earth high up in the atmosphere*

Water of life

Indian farmers rely heavily on monsoon rains to grow their crops. These rains are the only source of water for 70 percent of India's crops.

Ghat mountains

Spectacular clouds and torrential rains occur on the windward slopes of the Western Ghat mountains in India. There, the early monsoon winds pile up against the steep slopes until the wind and clouds eventually roll over the peaks and take the monsoon rains farther inland.

Rain dance

The monsoon rains are a cause for celebration when they first arrive. By this time, people have endured six months of brutally dry, oppressive weather and the cooling rains are a welcome relief.

"The best thing one can do when it's raining is to let it rain."

Henry Wadsworth Longfellow (1807–1882)
American poet

South Asian monsoon

The prevailing winds of summer blow from the Indian Ocean onto the warm Asian continent. In the winter, however, the prevailing winds blow outward from the cold land. The seasonal movement of the eastward-flowing jet stream also affects the monsoon winds. This high-level air stream blocks in warm, rising air, but the jet stream moves north in the summer, allowing moist ocean winds to be drawn farther into the continent.

KEY

1. Warm air rises off the baking land, drawing in a soft breeze from the cool ocean.

2. The eastward-flowing jet stream blocks in the rising air.

3. The jet stream moves north, allowing the warm air to rise unobstructed.

4. Water-laden winds stream in off the ocean.

5. Ocean winds forced over the mountains cool, bringing heavy rains on the coast.

6. Water-laden winds sweep northward, bringing rain to the rest of the country.

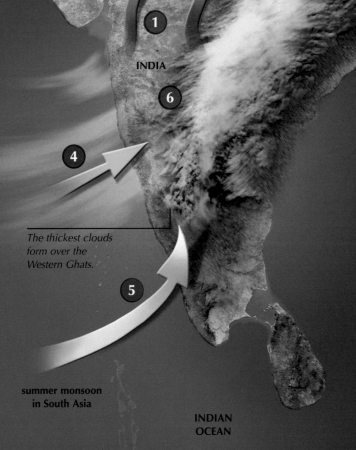

position of jet stream after it has moved north

3

HIMALAYA MOUNTAINS

2

position of jet stream in May

BANGLADESH

1

INDIA

6

4

The thickest clouds form over the Western Ghats.

5

summer monsoon in South Asia

INDIAN OCEAN

www.wrh.noaa.gov/fgz/science/monsoon.php?wfo=fgz

⊖ AFTER THE DELUGE

While farmers and those hoping for the end of the dry summer await the monsoon rains anxiously, the rains can also bring great hardship. They can be so intense that they cause floods, particularly in India and Bangladesh, where the delta of the Ganges River is at risk of frequent flooding, especially if a storm surge occurs at the same time.

Flooding in Bangladesh leaves communities in chaos.

DRY LANDS

The driest places on the planet are deserts. They are dry either because it simply does not rain very much or because the baking sun makes the air so warm that evaporation is greater than rainfall. It might surprise you to learn that polar regions are described as deserts. This is because the air there is too cold to hold enough moisture for precipitation. Without water, deserts become harsh, hostile environments, empty of all but a few plants and animals that are adapted to life in these conditions.

Night chills

By day, clear skies allow the Sun to scorch hot deserts. But with no clouds to trap the heat, the temperature may drop to below freezing at night, so desert-dwelling people must wrap up and build fires to stay warm.

Sahara scorcher

The Sahara is the world's largest hot desert. Its center is extremely arid (dry), with little vegetation. The highlands and northern and southern regions of the desert have areas of sparse grassland and desert shrubs. At noon, the temperature in the shade soars to more than 130°F (55°C). Few animals are active at this time. But as the Sun sets, many creatures emerge from under the rocks and out of their burrows.

> A region is called a desert if it usually receives 10 in. (25cm) or less of rain each year.

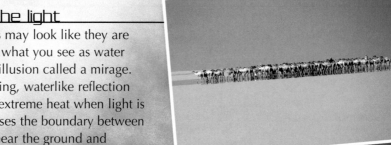

Trick of the light

These camels may look like they are drinking, but what you see as water is an optical illusion called a mirage. The shimmering, waterlike reflection is created in extreme heat when light is bent as it passes the boundary between very hot air near the ground and the slightly cooler air above it.

KEY

1 Rock pillars are carved into their unusual shapes by sand carried on the wind.

2 The sand cat uses any available cover to protect itself from the sun.

3 A cactus stores water in its swollen stem.

4 A desert eagle soars above the desert, watching for prey on the ground.

5 The fennec fox's burrowing and nocturnal lifestyle keeps it out of the baking sun.

6 The cape hare survives in higher temperatures than most other hares.

7 Strong winds blow sand and dust that sweep over the desert in a sandstorm.

8 The sidewinder snake uses a wavelike motion to move efficiently across the shifting sand.

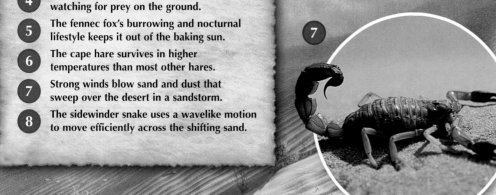

During the day, the Sahara scorpion hides under rocks to stay out of the sun.

⊖ DESERT DISTRIBUTION

Two large belts of desert regions, including those of the southwestern U.S., North Africa, and Australia, encircle the world in the subtropics on either side of the equator. Deserts formed in regions sheltered from the rain by high mountains include South America's Atacama Desert and Patagonia region and Asia's Taklimakan Desert. Parts of the Gobi Desert lie so deep in the Asian interior that winds bearing water from the oceans dry out before they reach the parched land.

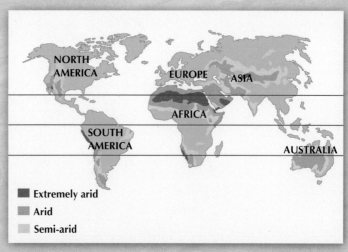

NORTH AMERICA EUROPE ASIA AFRICA SOUTH AMERICA AUSTRALIA

■ Extremely arid
■ Arid
■ Semi-arid

The world's deserts cover approximately one-third of the land.

WATER SHORTAGE

Many of us enjoy dry, sunny, cloudless days. However, unusually low rainfall for prolonged periods can lead to droughts. We expect to find dry, rainless conditions in very hot places between the tropics and the equator. But these conditions can also occur in regions that are too far inland for winds bearing moisture evaporated from the oceans to reach, or where mountains block winds from blowing moisture to the land beyond the peaks.

dust storm in
Melbourne, Australia

Black blizzard
When the wind blows hard over arid landscapes, it creates swirling clouds of choking, blinding sand and dust that can be carried on the wind for many miles. Dust storms in rural areas have been known to overwhelm whole cities.

Out of water
Crops cover swaths of the Midwest region of the U.S. If winds bearing moisture from the Gulf of Mexico in the south do not blow in the right direction, or with enough force, the crops can succumb to droughts.

⊖ SHIFTING STREAMS

Rivers of fast-moving winds, called jet streams, circle Earth in a meandering pattern high up in the atmosphere. Jet streams separate cold polar air from warmer air and change position with the seasons, moving tropical moisture to temperate regions. If there is a period when a jet stream weakens or follows a different path than usual, the moisture may be diverted away from where it is normally found. This results in a drought.

jet stream clouds over Egypt and the Red Sea

satellite view
of the Himalayas
and central Asia

"There struck the worst of dust storms that ever filled the sky . . . It fell across our city like a curtain of black rolled down."

Woody Guthrie (1912–1967)
American singer-songwriter, from his 1940 song
The Great Dust Storm

> During a dust storm in Australia in 2009, the country lost an estimated 82,700 tons of dust per hour to the Pacific Ocean.

www.cccok.org/museum/dustbowl.html

Parched land

The Taklimakan is a moderately warm, midlatitude desert. The region is far inland and ringed by mountains, so precipitation is extremely low, at about 0.95 in. (24mm) per year. Traditionally, camels were used to carry trade goods across this parched, sandy landscape because of the animals' ability to last long periods without water.

Lush vegetation covers
the rainy, windward side.

Arid conditions prevail
on the leeward side.

HIMALAYAS

A face scarf protects this
woman's eyes from dust as
she carries water in the Gobi
Desert, which is located in
the rain shadow of the
Himalayas.

Rain shadow

When winds meet mountains, the air rises to pass over the peaks. It becomes colder, causing rain to fall on that side of the mountain, known as the "windward" side. By the time the air makes it over the mountain to the "leeward" side, it has lost most of its vapor. This is known as the rain-shadow effect. It is one of the reasons why many deserts are found on the side of a mountain range facing away from the ocean.

La Niña,
January 1999

El Niño and La Niña

The unusually warm ocean created by an El Niño makes the air more humid, causing heavy rain and violent storms. Countries in the western Pacific, deprived of the warm ocean current, have very dry weather. La Niña tends to cause the opposite effects to El Niño. Where El Niño would cause a dry period, La Niña usually causes a rainy period.

"El Niño is similar to dropping a big rock in a pond; the pond in this case is the Pacific Ocean."

Jagadish Shukla (born 1944)
president of the Institute of Global Environment and Society, United States

PACIFIC PATTERNS

El Niño and La Niña are two extremes of a Pacific Ocean atmosphere cycle known as the El Niño-Southern Oscillation (ENSO). During an El Niño, the winds that blow west over the tropical Pacific Ocean weaken, allowing warm water to flow east. The westward-blowing winds become stronger during a La Niña, causing an abnormal amount of cold water to build up in the central and eastern Pacific. El Niño and La Niña dramatically affect world weather patterns, creating extreme conditions.

Down Under downpour

This fairground sits in a La Niña–related flood. La Niña events often bring above-average rainfall and floods to much of Australia. The tropical cyclone risk for northern Australia also increases at these times.

> El Niño, which is Spanish for "the boy," refers to baby Jesus because the unusual weather often begins around Christmas.

Turned to tinder

In times of drought, plants dry out and become more flammable, raising the risk of wildfires. During the 1999 La Niña–related drought in the U.S., 92,651 wildfires burned 5.7 million acres (2.3 million hectares) of land.

El Niño, October 1997

Coastal chaos

High winds and heavy rains, along with abnormally high tides, caused havoc in coastal California during the El Niño of the winter of 1997–1998.

KEY

1. The central and western U.S. are plagued by wildfires during a La Niña.

2. Warmer-than-usual water (shown in red and white) builds up in the western Pacific.

3. Cooler-than-usual water (shown in purple) builds up in the central and eastern Pacific.

4. Australia experiences heavy rainfall and flooding during a La Niña.

5. The western coast of the U.S. suffers El Niño–related storms that can cause surges and floods.

6. Cooler-than-usual water (shown in purple) builds up in the western Pacific.

7. Papua New Guinea endures droughts, which sometimes cause wildfires, during an El Niño.

8. Warmer-than-usual water (shown in red and white) builds up in the western Pacific.

9. Peru suffers severe storms during an El Niño.

http://kids.earth.nasa.gov/archive/nino/intro.html

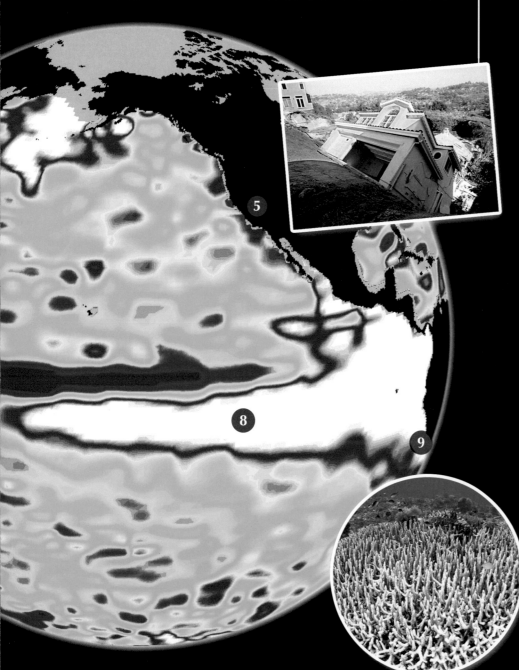

Freak floods

In the winter of 1997–1998, El Niño–related storms pummeled the coast of Peru, bringing heavy downpours even to places that had hardly seen rain in years. About 22,000 people fled their flooded homes, and mudslides buried entire villages.

Coral bleaching

Bleached, dead coral can indicate the presence of an El Niño. The tiny, colorful algae that live in coral survive only in certain temperatures. If the ocean's temperature is higher than normal, the algae moves away and the coral dies, leaving behind its pale "skeleton."

POLAR EXTREMES

The frozen polar regions at opposite ends of Earth receive less sunlight than anywhere else in the world. They are the coldest places on the planet. The southern region, Antarctica, is ravaged by hurricane-force winds, making it so inhospitable that the only humans who live there are scientists working in research stations. The Arctic in the north is slightly warmer, though bitterly cold compared with other places.

A weather balloon carries instruments up into the atmosphere to measure air pressure and temperature.

A face mask and goggles protect the researcher from the glare of the snow and blizzards.

Antarctic landscape and research station

Flagpoles are almost bent to the ground by the wind, which can reach up to 125 mph (200km/h).

Strong winds create a wind-chill, making the area feel colder than it actually is.

Extreme-cold clothing consists of windproof outer layers and under layers made of breathable materials.

 ❯ A total of 30 countries operate seasonal and permanent research stations in Antarctica.

Antarctic research

Scientists monitor Antarctica's weather and the sea ice because they affect the world's weather. Winds that constantly circle Antarctica drive storms across the ocean around it and beyond. In the winter, the surface of the ocean freezes, leaving behind salt. Some of the remaining water, heavy with salt, sinks and drives deep water currents in a system that carries ocean water around the world, redistributing heat.

Specially designed ships carry out research missions at sea and resupply the scientists on land with food and equipment.

www.antarcticconnection.com/antarctic/weather/climate.shtml

⊖ BEAR NECESSITIES

In the Arctic, large areas of once permanently frozen ocean have now become open water, with just a few scattered ice floes. Many scientists believe the ice is melting because of unusual increases in air temperature brought about by pollution in the atmosphere. Polar bears hunt from the ice, so they are now forced to swim exhausting distances to find stable ice from which they can secure food.

Polar bears hunt for food from ice floes in the Arctic Ocean.

Most of the snow that falls does not melt but acts like a mirror, reflecting many of the incoming solar rays back into space.

Dense plumage and a layer of fat under their skin keep penguins warm in the bitter cold.

SNOW HAZARDS

A snowy landscape may look magical, but snow can be deadly. Heavy snowfall can bury buildings or make roads impassable. Snow and strong winds cause blizzards, which reduce visibility, increasing the risk of accidents and people getting lost. Mountain snow can shift and crash down, wiping out skiers, trees, and even buildings.

Large cracks, called fissures, appear as a slab of snow begins to break away from its surroundings.

A snowflake's symmetrical shape can be seen through a microscope. No one has ever found two snowflakes that look the same.

Snowed in

Snow is mostly air, so it is light enough to be carried on the wind in drifts. The wind piles up drifts of snow against any obstacles, such as cabins, trains, and cars. These may become completely covered, trapping any people inside them.

> VISIBILITY—*the distance at which an object can be seen clearly*

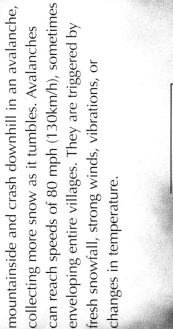

AvaLung

A search-and-rescue team digs out an avalanche survivor.

To the rescue

Teams use dogs and snow-probe poles to locate buried avalanche victims, but rescuers also rely on the survivors' use of beacons to summon the team to the right area. A person can last one hour completely buried if they breathe oxygen through an AvaLung breathing apparatus (above).

Whiteout

If snowstorms last for several hours and combine high winds with low visibility, the result is known as a blizzard. Blizzards can involve large amounts of falling snow or fallen snow that is whipped up by high winds.

Avalanche!

Snow can suddenly break loose on a steep mountainside and crash downhill in an avalanche, collecting more snow as it tumbles. Avalanches can reach speeds of 80 mph (130km/h), sometimes enveloping entire villages. They are triggered by fresh snowfall, strong winds, vibrations, or changes in temperature.

Rescuers carry transceivers that pick up signals from distress beacons.

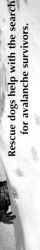

Rescue dogs help with the search for avalanche survivors.

> During the winter of 1951–1952, 649 avalanches in the European Alps killed about 265 people in what was known as the Winter of Terror.

Cloaked in clouds

During August, the Golden Gate Bridge, which spans San Francisco Bay in California, is draped in fog for most of the day. The fog forms when cold air—created by a cold-water current traveling south through the Pacific from the Arctic—rolls in from the ocean and mixes with warm summer air in the bay area. The cold air causes vapor in the warm air to condense into fog.

Clouds of smoke

"Smoke" plus "fog" makes "smog," such as in the days when fog mixed with smoke from coal-burning homes and factories. Today, smog is a mixture of air pollutants that hang in the air, usually around big cities. Smog can cause health problems, such as irritation to the eyes, nose, and throat. Long-term exposure to smog can lead to serious lung problems.

businessman wearing a mask to protect himself from smog in Tokyo, Japan

GROUND CLOUDS

Unless they have radar, ships must move cautiously or not at all in fog.

It is possible that you have literally had your head in the clouds without realizing it, as fog is a type of cloud. It forms near the ground when the air is full of moisture and the temperature drops. If you cannot see beyond 3,300 ft. (1,000m) through the suspended particles of moisture, the obstruction is considered to be fog. Otherwise, it is called mist. Sometimes, what appears to be thick fog in the air is, in fact, a much more sinister haze called smog.

 > The Grand Banks off the island of Newfoundland, Canada, is the foggiest place in the world, with more than 200 foggy days a year.

"Fair is foul, and foul is fair: hover through the fog and filthy air."

William Shakespeare (1564–1616)
English playwright, from his play Macbeth

Delayed departures

Aircraft are at their most vulnerable during takeoff and landing, when the scope for making unplanned maneuvers is limited. So when visibility is severely reduced because of fog at an airport, planes are grounded. Any aircraft trying to land there are diverted to a fog-free airport.

Hill fog

Low clouds that sit below the top of hills or mountains are known as hill fog or upslope fog. This is formed as mild, moist air meets a hill or mountain obstacle and is forced to climb up it. As the air moves up, it cools down, causing the moisture in the air to condense and form clouds.

Treacherous travel

In very thick fog, you may not be able to see beyond a few yards. Traveling in conditions such as these is very dangerous, and accidents are common. Most ships and aircraft use radar to locate their position in relation to other craft. The fog-penetrating light from lighthouses warns ships away from rocks.

Shrouded in fog, the light from a lighthouse guides ships to safety.

⊖ FOG COLLECTORS

Although the northern coast of Chile is enveloped in a shroud of thick cloud, known locally as *camanchaca*, the cloud does not have enough moisture to produce rain, and the region is extremely dry. Some villages have put up fog nets to collect the fog water. The nets are supported by a post at either end and are positioned at a right angle to the wind. Water droplets collect on the net and fall under the force of gravity into a gutter. This directs the water into a storage tank, from where the villagers can collect the water.

Water-collection nets in Chungungo provide the villagers with a water supply.

WEATHER WATCH

DOPPLER RADAR—an instrument that uses radio waves to measure the speed and direction of a moving object

Hurricanes and other extreme weather events cannot be prevented, but with warning, people may have time to protect themselves, their animals, and their property. The meteorological measurements used to predict extreme weather come from a wide range of sources, such as land-based weather stations, sea-based research ships, floating weather buoys, airborne balloons, and specially designed aircraft. Satellites out in space beam back pictures, monitor temperature and cloud patterns, and even measure wave heights.

⊖ RADAR RAIN MAP

A special type of Doppler radar is used to probe storm clouds. Raindrops, snow crystals, and hailstones within the clouds reflect some of the radio waves back to the radar, which converts them into maps such as this one. The precipitation type is indicated by colors, which are shown here in the scale on the right. Looking down the scale, the colors indicate increasingly heavy precipitation: green is light rain, white is heavy rain, and the bottom colors are hail.

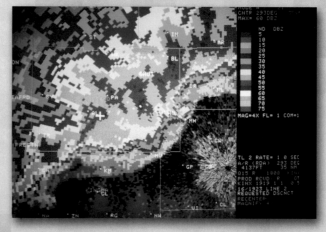

a color map of rain data generated by Doppler radar

Thousands of land-based stations feed information to 13 central weather centers.

Engineers install weather buoys with equipment that transmits readings back to the land via satellites.

The first weather satellite, *Vanguard 2*, was launched in 1959.

http://www.fema.gov/kids/huhunt.htm

Hurricane hunter

When dangerous-looking storm clouds appear, hurricane-hunting pilots take to the skies, flying over and even through storms and hurricanes. Equipment onboard the aircraft takes pictures and measurements inside the storms. Often, the crew drops mini weather stations on parachutes into the eye wall to measure conditions such as temperature, humidity, and wind speed at different heights.

Some research aircraft fly straight through the eye of a storm.

Scientists on board the aircraft use specialist equipment to navigate their way through storms, recording data as they go.

Hurricane surveillance

A developing hurricane is under constant observation by satellites in space, special aircraft, and Doppler radar on the ground. Satellite images show the path of a hurricane. Meanwhile, the radar provides information for estimating rainfall and monitors the bands of rain, the hurricane's eye, and the eye wall around it (see illustration on page 17). The aircraft gather data on air pressure and storm size. In addition, buoys floating on the oceans relay information about water temperatures that could fuel the hurricane.

"Prediction is very hard, especially when it is about the future."

Lawrence Peter "Yogi" Berra (born 1925)
American baseball legend

CARBON DIOXIDE—*a colorless, odorless gas formed when carbon combines with oxygen*

Melting away

In only five weeks during the Antarctic summer of 2002, a 1,200–sq. mi. (3,200-km^2) section of the Larsen B ice shelf broke up and floated into the Weddell Sea as icebergs. The 720-ft. (220-m)-thick mass of floating ice had been stable for 12,000 years before its collapse. This was caused by increasing temperatures in the region, which has seen a 4.5°F (2.5°C) temperature rise over the past 50 years.

Larsen B shelf on January 31, 2002

The ice shelf is a floating extension of an ice sheet on land.

Coal

During the past 100 years or so, we have enjoyed a technological revolution powered by fossil fuels, especially coal. When they are burned, fossil fuels release carbon dioxide into the atmosphere.

CLIMATE CHANGE

Clues to the climates of the distant past can be found in rocks, fossils, and the polar ice sheets. These show that throughout Earth's history there were times that, when averaged, world surface temperatures were either lower or higher than today's average. The past 100 years have seen an unusually rapid increase in the average global temperature. This is known as global warming, and it seems to coincide with an increase in carbon-dioxide emissions created by human activity. Many scientists predict that global warming could have catastrophic effects.

 About 90 percent of the world's ice is on Antarctica. Global sea levels would rise by 200 ft. (61m) if this ice melted.

Bird's-eye view

NASA launched the NOAA-6 weather satellite in 1979. It has been instrumental in the mapping of ice in the polar regions ever since it was delivered into orbit. The maps provide a vivid record of the deterioration of the polar icecaps as a result of climate change.

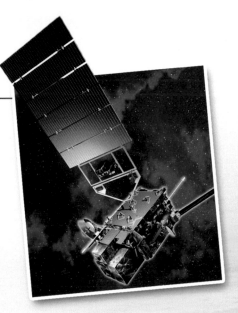

Rising sea levels

Some scientists predict that global warming could make Earth's climate about 4.5°F (2.5°C) warmer during the 21st century. This heat could cause seawater to warm up and expand, raising sea levels. If this happens, many islands that lie only 3–6.5 ft. (1–2m) above sea level could simply disappear.

Funafuti Island in the Pacific Ocean

Scientists use a hollow drill bit to extract the ice core.

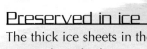

Preserved in ice

The thick ice sheets in the polar regions have built up over thousands of years. Pockets of air and particles of pollen and dust, trapped in the ice when it first formed, provide valuable information about past climates. This information helps scientists make predictions about future climates. Researchers use drills to extract columns, or cores, of ice from the ice sheets for analysis.

www.globalchange.gov

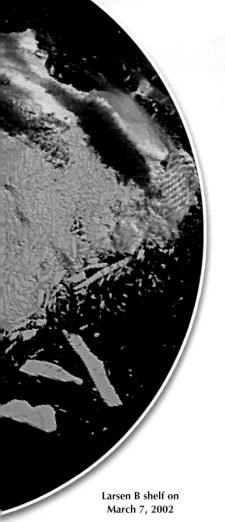

Larsen B shelf on March 7, 2002

● UPS AND DOWNS

During most of Earth's history, the planet was warmer than it is now, but with icy periods in between called ice ages. Most of these climate changes developed naturally and over extremely long periods of time. However, the past century has seen an average global air-temperature rise of almost 1.4°F (0.8°C), which is dramatic if you consider that the world has warmed by only 7°F (4°C) in the past 2,000 years.

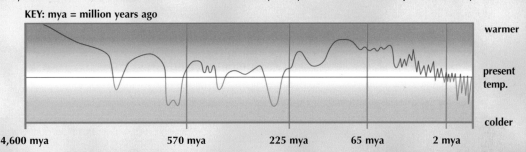

KEY: mya = million years ago

warmer

present temp.

colder

| 4,600 mya | 570 mya | 225 mya | 65 mya | 2 mya |

CLEANUP

First, workers rescue survivors trapped under ruins by carefully clearing rubble by hand and with diggers. If there is flooding, the emergency services use powerful pumps to drain the excess water. Later, the debris is cleared and buildings are made safe. Bridges and roads are rebuilt to allow easy movement in and out of the sites so that reconstruction can begin fully.

rescuing trapped survivors

draining floodwater with a pump

reconstructing bridges and roads

DISASTER RELIEF

Weather-related disasters such as tornadoes, hurricanes, and mudslides are usually over in a few minutes in a given location. But it can take months or even years to repair the damage they cause. When extreme weather strikes, relief workers race to the affected area and immediately set about searching for survivors among the ruined buildings. Injured people are rushed to hospitals, while other survivors are given shelter, water, and food. Over time, the debris is cleared and buildings are reconstructed.

Tents and living equipment were provided for these victims of the 1984 Ethiopian drought.

Water tanks
Even during a flood, when water is everywhere, clean drinking water is often in short supply. Relief workers must install temporary water tanks to provide fresh and safe drinking water for those who need it.

Temporary homes
One of the first concerns of relief workers is to provide shelter for those left without homes by the disaster. The homeless may be temporarily housed together in a large building, or each family may be provided with a tent and essential survival equipment, such as blankets, matches, and food.

> STAPLE FOOD—*the main food eaten and the main source of energy in someone's diet*

Emergency supplies

If disaster strikes a remote or inaccessible location, the quickest way to get aid there is usually to drop it from the sky. Where possible, relief workers seal off a drop zone to ensure that the falling packages do not injure people on the ground. The packages contain staple foods, such as wheat, flour, rice, beans, and powdered milk. Sometimes, the packages also contain medical supplies and blankets.

Armed forces personnel and equipment are usually called in to help with the relief effort.

Helicopters can make more precise drops than aircraft.

Flood victims rush for food packages in Andhra Pradesh state, India, in 2009.

Protective packaging cushions the box's contents from the force of impact with the ground.

> In 2007, the EU and its member states gave $1.1 billion in emergency relief, making the EU the world's largest aid donor.

DAMAGE LIMITATION

Hurricanes, tornadoes, and other extreme weather events cannot be prevented, but the damage they cause can be limited. Weather centers broadcast warnings so that people can take refuge in specially designed shelters, or even leave the region if they can. Flood- and avalanche-management strategies often involve the creation of barriers that are designed to hold back the deluge, preventing it from reaching settlements and people. Some of these defenses are inspired by those found in nature.

FLOOD BARRIER—a series of adjustable gates or a movable wall for closing off a watercourse to protect it from a storm surge

Dune planting

Sand dunes protect coasts from storm surges, while vegetation on the dunes keeps them stable. Dune plants damaged by beach users and grazing animals are replaced as part of coastal protection projects, such as the one shown here.

Hurricane shelter

About three-fourths of the southern Asian country of Bangladesh is only 33 ft. (10m) above sea level. Flooding is frequent, especially during the monsoon season between June and September and the typhoon (hurricane) season of August through November. Some communities have built large shelters, which are raised above the ground on stilts so that floodwaters can pass beneath them. The shelters are also designed to withstand hurricane-force winds.

hurricane shelter in Bangladesh

> The Thames Barrier closed four times in the 1980s, 35 times in the 1990s, and 75 times in the first decade of this century.

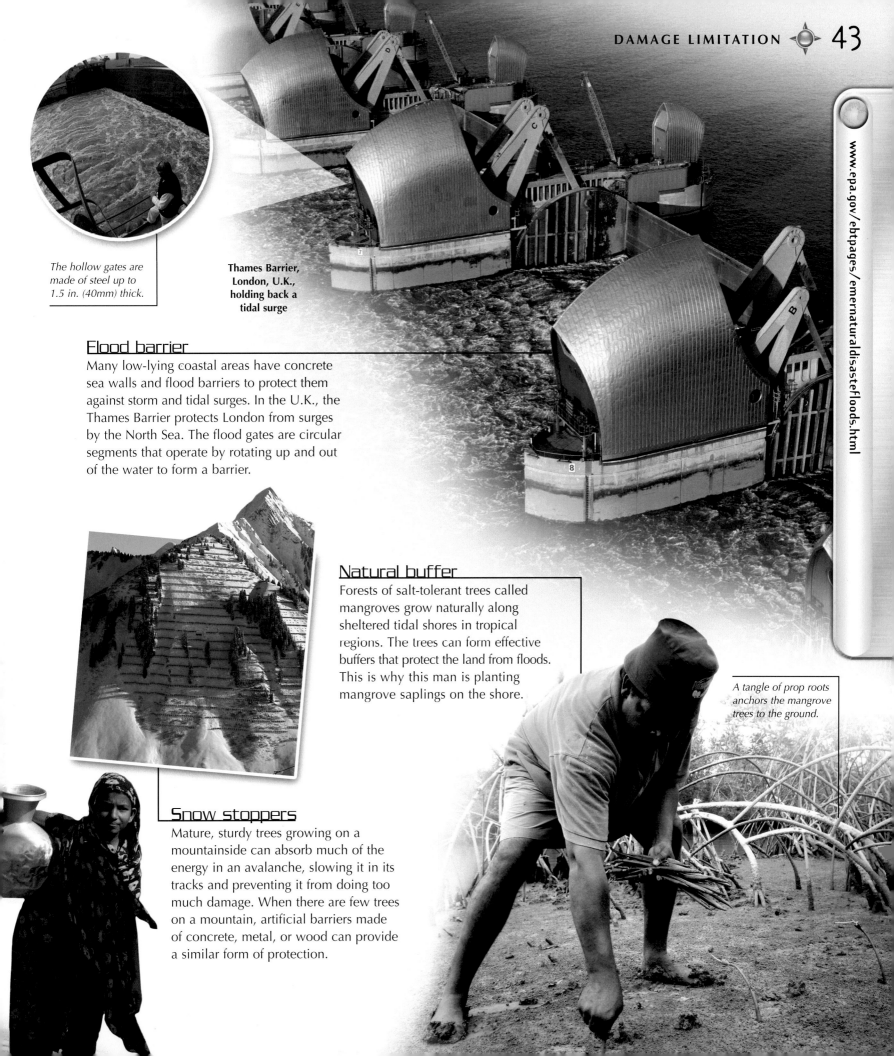

The hollow gates are made of steel up to 1.5 in. (40mm) thick.

Thames Barrier, London, U.K., holding back a tidal surge

www.epa.gov/ebtpages/emernaturaldisastefloods.html

Flood barrier

Many low-lying coastal areas have concrete sea walls and flood barriers to protect them against storm and tidal surges. In the U.K., the Thames Barrier protects London from surges by the North Sea. The flood gates are circular segments that operate by rotating up and out of the water to form a barrier.

Natural buffer

Forests of salt-tolerant trees called mangroves grow naturally along sheltered tidal shores in tropical regions. The trees can form effective buffers that protect the land from floods. This is why this man is planting mangrove saplings on the shore.

A tangle of prop roots anchors the mangrove trees to the ground.

Snow stoppers

Mature, sturdy trees growing on a mountainside can absorb much of the energy in an avalanche, slowing it in its tracks and preventing it from doing too much damage. When there are few trees on a mountain, artificial barriers made of concrete, metal, or wood can provide a similar form of protection.

GLOSSARY

avalanche
A mass of loose snow moving rapidly down a mountainside.

climate
The normal pattern of weather in a region over a long period of time.

climate change
This occurs when Earth's climate is remarkably altered as a result of natural causes or human activities.

cloud
A visible mass of condensed water vapor or ice particles (or both) suspended in the sky.

condense
To change from a gas into a liquid.

cumulonimbus
A tall, dark cloud that produces heavy rain, hail, and thunderstorms.

current
A ribbon of flowing ocean water.

cyclone
The name for a hurricane in the South Pacific and Indian oceans.

desert
A landscape that receives very little precipitation.

downdraft
A sinking current of air.

drought
Below average rainfall over an extended period of time.

equator
An imaginary line around the middle of Earth. It separates the Northern and Southern Hemispheres.

evaporate
To change from a liquid into a gas.

eye
The calm, usually cloud-free center of a hurricane.

flash flood
A flood that rises very quickly after a rainstorm.

fog
Water that has condensed from vapor into tiny droplets suspended in the air, close to the ground.

global warming
A long-term increase in the global average temperature.

hail
Rounded drops of ice that fall to the ground from storm clouds.

hemisphere
One half of Earth. There is a northern and a southern hemisphere.

hurricane
A powerful storm that forms over the tropical parts of oceans. In different parts of the world, it is called a cyclone or a typhoon.

ice
Water that gets so cold that it freezes.

ice age
One of several periods in Earth's history when ice sheets covered a large part of the planet's surface.

ice sheet
A thick layer of ice that covers a very large area.

lightning
A flash of electricity in the sky.

monsoon

A seasonal change of wind that affects the weather, especially in tropical areas, where it causes wet and dry seasons.

pack ice

A large expanse of floating ice, usually at the poles.

pollution

Anything that makes air, water, or the land unpleasant or unhealthy for living things.

precipitation

Moisture released from the air in the form of rain, snow, hail, fog, or dew.

prevailing winds

The main direction from which winds usually blow in a certain place.

rain

Drops of water that fall from a cloud.

rain band

A long line of continuous cloud that releases heavy rain.

rain shadow

An area of decreased rainfall on the leeward, or sheltered, side of a mountain or hill.

snow

Precipitation falling from clouds in the form of clusters of ice crystals. The crystals freeze directly from vapor without turning into raindrops.

subtropics

The regions of Earth that lie just to the north of the Tropic of Capricorn and just to the south of the Tropic of Cancer.

supercell

A very large thundercloud with a constant rotating updraught in the middle. Supercells often produce large hail, powerful downpours, very strong winds, and sometimes tornadoes.

thunder

The sound made by air as it expands during a flash of lightning.

tornado

A violent, rotating column of air that is in contact with both the ground and a cumulonimbus cloud.

trade winds

Steady, easterly winds that blow from the tropics toward the equator.

tropics

The hot regions to the north and south of the equator, between the Tropic of Cancer and the Tropic of Capricorn.

typhoon

The name given to a hurricane in Japan.

updraft

A rising current of air.

waterspout

A column of spiraling air that travels across water.

water vapor

The invisible gas that forms when water evaporates.

weather

The conditions of the atmosphere at a certain time and place.

wind

The movement of air from one place to another.

INDEX

INDEX

INVESTIGATE

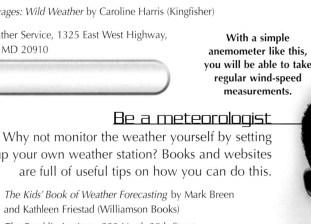

We know extreme weather can be deadly, so it is always best to avoid firsthand experience with it. Find out how meteorologists predict extreme weather—and what people can do to protect themselves from it—by checking out weather centers, museums, websites, and books.

Extreme weather defenses

There are weather defenses all around you, such as ocean and river walls, flood barriers, sand dunes, and coastal plants.

a meteorologist showing a visitor how he converts weather data into charts

 Wonders of the World by Philip Steele (Kingfisher)

 Museum of American Weather, South Common, Haverhill, NH 03765

www.nhc.noaa.gov

Try taking part in an organized dune-planting project like this one (above).

Watch the experts

Arrange to visit a weather center, where you can see experts at work. You can also ask them questions and find out how you can get involved in weather research.

 Kingfisher Voyages: Wild Weather by Caroline Harris (Kingfisher)

 National Weather Service, 1325 East West Highway, Silver Spring, MD 20910

www.weather.gov

With a simple anemometer like this, you will be able to take regular wind-speed measurements.

Be a meteorologist

Why not monitor the weather yourself by setting up your own weather station? Books and websites are full of useful tips on how you can do this.

 The Kids' Book of Weather Forecasting by Mark Breen and Kathleen Friestad (Williamson Books)

 The Franklin Institute, 222 North 20th Street, Philadelphia, PA 19103

www.bwca.cc/weather/weatherblueprints.htm

Webcams broadcast live images from the research stations.

Antarctic research

You don't have to endure subzero temperatures and blizzards to find out about Antarctic research. Simply follow the day-to-day activities of scientists online.

 Antarctica: Secrets of the Southern Continent by David McGonigal (Firefly Books)

 Ice Station Antarctica, Natural History Museum, Cromwell Road, London SW7 5BD, U.K.

www.antarctica.ac.uk/images/webcams/index.php